AF480040

THE WORLD'S MOST BEAUTIFUL BIRDS!

Animal Book for Toddlers
Children's Animal Books

Speedy Publishing LLC

40 E. Main St. #1156

Newark, DE 19711

www.speedypublishing.com

Copyright 2017

Birds are mainly pretty to impress other birds. But we can enjoy them, too! Which are your favorite birds? Let's look at some lovely birds from around the world.

VERMILION FLYCATCHER BIRD
EATING INSECT

THE BIRDS AMONG US

Birds are an essential part of the community of life on Earth. They help plants spread their seeds, they eat insects, and they themselves make meals for larger creatures.

Normally male birds of a species are much more colorful than females, and they use their bright colors and pretty designs to help find a female bird to have babies with. For a few species, like penguins, the males and females look pretty much the same. But usually the male is a little larger and a lot more colorful!

KING PENGUIN

KINGFISHER

Some birds, like seagulls, show up all around the Earth. Some of the most beautiful birds fall into that category:

KINGFISHER

The kingfisher's dramatic shape and coloring, and the fact that you often find them in a pretty scene, means that photographers love to take pictures of this bird all around the world.

Most species, however, have their home in a particular part of the world, or in a particular climate. Let's take a world tour of beautiful birds!

BIRDS OF SOUTH AMERICA

Here are some birds you mainly find in South America.

HYACINTH MACAW

This macaw is the largest flying parrot in the world. It lives in open areas and grasslands in northern Brazil. There are very few left in the world because of hunting, and because their habitat is getting smaller as people expand farms and build roads.

TWO HYACINTH MACAWS
SITTING ON A PALM TREE

GREEN WING MACAWS

The macaw has bright blue feathers with yellow rings around the eyes. They are sometimes called "blue macaws". When they are talking together, the macaws can be very loud!

GREEN WING MACAW

This macaw lives all over Central and South America, in forests, open land, and mangrove swamps.

RED-NECKED TANAGER

Tanagers have wings with many bright colors. They live in rainforests in the lowlands of Brazil, Argentina, and Paraguay.

SPANGLED COTINGA

The continga is so beautiful that it is in danger because hunters want to catch it for its feathers. It does not sing, but when it flies, its wings make a whistling sound.

VIOLET-CROWNED WOODNYMPH

This is a tiny bird, just four inches long. Its shiny purple and green feather look like they are made of metal. It lives in moist lowland forests, and in lands that were forests, but have been clear-cut and are growing back.

CURL-CRESTED ARACARI

This toucan has feathers on its head that look like the ribbons on a Christmas present! As many as five adults and all their young children share the same nest. They live in moist lowland forests of Peru, Brazil, and Bolivia.

PARADISE TANAGER

This songbird lives in the Amazon River Basin. The tanagers live in groups of twenty or more birds, and travel in flocks to eat or drink.

ANDEAN COCK-OF-THE-ROCK

This bird has remarkable orange feathers on its face, giving a contrast to its dark eyes. The males have an impressive crest of feathers on their heads.

BIRDS OF AFRICA

If you travel to Africa, you may see these birds, among many other amazing animals!

HYACINTH MACAW

This bird lives in Africa, but many have been sold in the United States as pets.

HYACINTH MACAW

AFRICAN CROWNED CRANE

This lovely crane lives in the African savanna, and sometimes in the southern part of the Sahara Desert. However, they are not really desert birds: they like cool, wet climates.

Learn more about where they live in the Baby Professor book Ecosystem Facts That You Should Know - The Savanna and Tundra Edition.

MASKED LOVEBIRDS

YELLOW-COLLARED LOVEBIRD

These birds are green and yellow, and very small members of the parrot family. They are sometimes called "masked lovebirds" because of the rings around their eyes. Their home is in Tanzania, in the east of Africa.

YELLOW-BREASTED ROLLER

These lovely birds live in open woodland south of the Sahara Desert. Both Kenya and Botswana consider the yellow-breasted roller their national bird.

BIRDS OF ASIA

When you travel to Asia or the islands of the Pacific Ocean, you may see one of these birds in the sky over your head:

STORK-BILLED KINGFISHER

These birds live in the tropical forests of southern Asia, especially in India and Sri Lanka. They are so beautiful that bird-watchers travel long distances to see them.

STORK-BILLED KINGFISHER

GOLDEN PHEASANT

The golden pheasant lives in the forests of western China, especially in the mountains. It is very popular because it is so beautiful.

BALI BIRD OF PARADISE

Bali is an island in Indonesia, and its bird of paradise is very hard to see. They live in remote areas of the rainforest, and you will probably only see them in photographs or videos, or in a zoo.

RED-BEARDED BEE EATER

This bird lives in clearings in the dense forests of Indonesia and Malaya. It happily eats wasps, hornets, and all sorts of other insects, as well as bees.

LADY GOULDIAN FINCH

LADY GOULDIAN FINCH

This Australian bird is also known as the "rainbow finch" for its bright feathers. There are fewer than three thousand of these finches left in the wild because of hunting, and because human activity has made their habitat smaller, but many are raised in captivity to be sold as pets.

Artist John Gould named this species after his wife, Elizabeth, in 1844.

WESTERN CROWNED PIGEON

This pigeon has remarkable crests on its head and a mask of blue feathers around its eyes. It lives in Papua New Guinea, and some nearby islands. People hunt the pigeon for its feathers, and as food, and it only survives in areas that are hard for people to visit.

WESTERN CROWNED PIGEON

SPLENDID FAIRY WREN

This lovely blue bird lives all across Asia and Australia. The males collect flower petals and display them to attract and impress the females.

CRIMSON ROSELLA

This is perhaps the most famous parrot species. It has bright blue and red feathers and a very loud voice! It lives in forests and woodlands of eastern Australia, eating mainly seeds, fruits, and herbs.

RAINBOW LORIKEET

The rainbow lorikeet lives in eastern Australia and in Tasmania. It prefers living in rainforests or wooded areas along the coast.

MANDARIN DUCK

Mandarin ducks live throughout east Asia. They are "perching ducks", and like to sit on tree branches. The males have gorgeous feathers, and the females have a bright white eye ring that contrasts with the brown feathers of the rest of their bodies.

BLUE-CROWNED PENGUIN

We think of penguins in Antarctica, but species like the blue-crowned penguin live in warmer waters. This amazing-looking bird has its home in New Zealand.

Learn more about penguins who are far from the South Pole in the Baby Professor book Penguins Like Warm Climates, too!

WOODDUCK

BIRDS OF NORTH AND CENTRAL AMERICA

In North and Central America, you might see one of these birds outside your window:

WOOD DUCK

This may be the most beautiful waterbird on Earth. The male bird's feathers shine like metal, and its neck has lovely white stripes.

The female has feathers that are less bright than the males, as is typical for most birds.

Wood ducks live in wetlands and swamps, and along rivers and streams. They nest in holes in trees and they gather in flocks, which is not typical of most water birds.

KEEL-BILLED TOUCAN

Belize considers the keel-billed toucan its national bird. It has bright blue feet, and red feathers in its tail.

QUETZAL

The quetzal lives in the forests and mountains of Central America. It lives on fruit, lizards, and insects. In ancient times, the Native Americans of Central America thought the quetzal was a god. Its name means "precious" or "sacred" in several languages of the region.

TURQUOISE-BROWED MOTMOT

TURQUOISE-BROWED MOTMOT

This bird has remarkable bright feathers. It lives in many countries of Central America, but both El Salvador and Nicaragua consider it their national bird.

PAINTED BUNTING

The painted bunting lives in many areas of North America. It has a blue head, and an orange body with a green back.

BROAD-BILLED HUMMINGBIRD

Hummingbirds are tiny, like flying jewels. Their wings move so fast you can barely see them. Hummingbirds live in North American during the warmer parts of the year, and then migrate to Central America or even South America to avoid the cold of winter.

PURPLE GALLINULE

PURPLE GALLINULE

This bird, with its bright plumage, lives in the southeast of the United States. It eats plants, insects, and fish, making it an "omnivore".

NORTHERN CARDINAL

Cardinals flit among the trees in forests and swamps all across the United States, Canada, and Mexico. They have a bright crest of feathers on the top of their heads.

CARDINAL IN SNOW

NORTHERN ORIOLE

NORTHERN ORIOLE

The northern oriole lives in woodlands of the eastern United States. Many people know its distinctive orange body because it is the mascot of a professional baseball team.

BIRDS ARE PART OF THE FAMILY OF EARTH

Whether they are beautiful or clothed in more quiet colors, all the creatures of Earth deserve our love and respect.

Find out about more creatures, from those that swim in the sea to those that roam the land, in Baby Professor books like The Great White Shark, Just Keep Swimming!, Insects and Arachnids, and Dogs and Cats.

Visit
BABY PROFESSOR
EDUCATION KIDS
www.BabyProfessorBooks.com
to download Free Baby Professor eBooks and view
our catalog of new and exciting Children's Books